MOVING MOUNTAINS

JOHN ELDREDGE

MOVING MOUNTAINS

Praying with Passion,
Confidence, and Authority

STUSY GUIDE | EIGHT SESSIONS

NELSON
BOOKS

An Imprint of Thomas Nelson

RANSOMED HEART
LOVE GOD. LIVE FREE.

RANSOMEDHEART.COM

Published in Nashville, Tennessee, by Nelson Books, an imprint of Thomas Nelson. Nelson Books and Thomas Nelson are registered trademarks of HarperCollins Christian Publishing, Inc.

Published in association with Yates & Yates, www.yates2.com.

Unless otherwise indicated, all Scripture quotations are taken from The Holy Bible, *New International Version*®, *NIV*®. Copyright © 1973, 1978, 1984 by Biblica, Inc.® Used by permission. All rights reserved worldwide.

Scripture quotations marked UPDATED NIV are taken from The Holy Bible, *New International Version*®, *NIV*® Copyright © 1973, 1978, 1984, 2011 by Biblica, Inc.® Used by permission. All rights reserved worldwide.

Scripture quotations marked MSG are taken from *The Message* by Eugene H. Peterson. © 1993, 1994, 1995, 1996, 2000. Used by permission of NavPress Publishing Group. All rights reserved.

Thomas Nelson titles may be purchased in bulk for educational, business, fund-raising, or sales promotional use. For information, please e-mail SpecialMarkets@ThomasNelson.com.

ISBN 978-0-7180-3849-6

First Printing February 2016 / Printed in the United States of America

CONTENTS

INTRODUCTION

You are about to embark on a wonderful adventure with God.

Really.

To draw closer to God in prayer, discover how he is at work, and join him in his Great Mission through the power of truly effective prayer—what could be more thrilling? As I say in *Moving Mountains*, "There is nothing more hopeful than the thought that things can be different, we *can* move mountains, and we have some role in bringing that change about."

Now *that's* exciting!

This study guide is meant to be a companion to the book *Moving Mountains* and the eight sessions you'll be watching in the video series. (You'll want to have a copy of the book and a copy of the video. If you are leading a group, we have provided a leader's guide in the back of this study.) I have combined two chapters of the book into each "session" in this guide, making this an eight-part study. So, you will be covering two chapters in the book each time you do the videos or use this study.

Each session in this guide will have three parts:

1. **Personal Preparation:** Before your group meets (we're assuming you are doing this in a group—though you could also do this study on your own), you'll want to read the corresponding chapters in the book and answer a few questions in this guide.

2. **Group Discussion:** Watch the session video as a group, take some notes, and then talk about it. In this section we've suggested a few questions to help guide your group's conversation time. (Again, if you are a leader, there's more guidance for you in the leader's guide at the back of the study guide.)

3. **Prayer Exercise:** The best way to grow in prayer is to actually engage in prayer. So, each week you will be given a "prayer project" to help you practice the concepts you've learned during the session.

Whatever your experience of prayer has been, whatever the ups and downs, I believe you will find this very refreshing, and hopeful; I believe you will see answers to prayer! So let's take the journey together as we ask Jesus—as his disciples did—"teach us to pray" (Luke 11:1).

THERE IS A WAY THINGS WORK

We just want [prayer] to be simple and easy. . . . The problem is,
sometimes [God] comes through, often he doesn't, and we have no idea
for the rhyme or reason why. We lose heart and abandon prayer.
(And we feel hurt and justified in doing so.) We abandon the very treasure
God has given us for not losing heart, for moving the "mountains"
in front of us, bringing about the changes we so desperately want to
see in our world. The uncomfortable truth is this: that is a very naïve view
of prayer, on a level with believing that all a marriage needs is love,
or that we should base our foreign policy on belief in our fellow man.
That simple view of prayer has crushed many a dear soul,
because it ignores crucial facts. There is a way things work.

JOHN ELDREDGE

PERSONAL PREPARATION

This week, read chapters 1 and 2 in *Moving Mountains:* "Prayer That Works" and "Third Graders at Normandy." Let's begin simply and honestly with your reaction to these first two chapters. Our first reaction is often a telling one, revealing places and assumptions in us that God wants to speak to. So, without any pressure to get the "answer right," what did this stir in you?

Prayer That Works

» Right up front, I confess that we all have a mixed story with prayer—prayers answered, prayers unanswered, and silence we can't quite make sense of. What is your story with prayer? To begin with, do you pray much? Why or why not?

» Can you recall a few stories of answered prayer? If so, what were they?

» And what about unanswered prayer—what have you been praying about that seems to as of yet have no answers?

» What have you done with unanswered prayer? (Gotten mad, given up, lost heart, stopped praying, kept at it like the persistent widow?)

» In chapter 1, I said that most people approach prayer like this:

> We just want it to be simple and easy; we want it to go like this: God is loving and powerful. We need his help. So we ask for help, as best we know how. The rest is up to him. After all—he's God. He can do anything (*Moving Mountains*, page 5).

Does that pretty much sum up the way you'd like prayer to work? Why or why not?

» One of the big ideas in chapter 1 is that *there is a way things work—even in prayer*. In what ways has that been part of your understanding of prayer?

» After recounting the story of Elijah praying to end the three-year drought, I said this:

> I love this narrative; it is so practical, and immensely helpful when it comes to understanding prayer and how it works. God is going to come through alright, but he insists

on involving Elijah's prayers. It reminds me of Augustine's line, "Without God, we cannot, and without us, he will not." We find ourselves in the sort of universe where prayer plays a crucial role, sometimes, the deciding role. Our choices matter (page 9).

The story of the way Elijah prayed to end the drought—how would that compare to the way you have traditionally approached prayer?

The brother of Jesus is giving his readers a tutorial on the subject of prayer. (He had seen some serious demonstrations of prayer, we might recall, growing up around the man who turned a boy's lunch into an all-you-can-eat buffet for five thousand.) James points to the famous drought story I just cited, then makes a staggering connection—you are no different than Elijah. That was his purpose in using the phrase, "Elijah was a man just like us." James was trying to disarm that religious posture that so often poisons the value of biblical stories: *Well, sure, that was so-and-so* [in this case Elijah] *and they were different than us.* Nope. Not the case. Actually, James makes it very clear: Elijah was a human being just like you. In other words, *you can do it too* (page 11).

» What do you make of the idea that James says, "You can do it too"?

Third Graders in Normandy

» There are two big ideas in chapter 2. The first is simply this: *God is growing us all up.*

> . . . until we all reach unity in the faith and in the knowledge of the Son of God and become mature . . . (Ephesians 4:13).

> . . . wrestling in prayer for you, that you may stand firm in all the will of God, mature and fully assured (Colossians 4:12).

> Brothers, stop thinking like children (1 Corinthians 14:20).

> Therefore let us leave the elementary teachings about Christ and go on to maturity, not laying again the foundation of repentance from acts that lead to death, and of faith in God, instruction about baptisms, the laying on of hands, the resurrection of the dead, and eternal judgment (Hebrews 6:1–2).

The call to grow up is very clear. "And how does God provide for growing us up? What are his *means*? Situations that stretch us, strain us, push us beyond what we thought we could endure—those very same circumstances that cause us to pray" (page 16). How has "growing up" been central to your understanding of what God is up to in your life?

» How might your assumptions about that affect your prayer life?

This assumption is important for one simple reason: it changes your expectations. When you show up at the gym, you are not surprised or irritated that the trainer pushes you into a drenching sweat; it's what you came for. But you'd be furious if your housemate expected this of you when you flop home on the couch after a long day's work. (Perhaps you might begin to see the connection in some of your feelings toward God) (page 16).

» *Do* you see the connection? Explain.

» The second big idea in chapter 2 is this: *We are at war.* We were born into a great battle.

The Scriptures are a sort of wake-up call to the human race, a trumpet blast, to use Francis Thompson's phrase, "from this hid battlements of eternity."[1] One alarm they repeatedly sound is that we are all caught up in the midst of a collision of kingdoms—the kingdom of God advancing with force against the kingdom of darkness, which for the moment holds most of the world in its clutches. Is this your understanding of the world you find yourself in? Does this shape the way you pray—and the way you interpret "unanswered" prayer? (page 20).

Has this been true of your basic convictions of the world? If not, why not?

» How might it change your prayer life if you did hold as one of your deepest beliefs that you live in a world at war?

THE BIG IDEAS

» There is a way things work—even in prayer.
» God is growing us all up—through situations that stretch us, strain us, and push us beyond what we thought we could endure.
» We are at war—a collision between the kingdom of God advancing with force against the kingdom of darkness.

GROUP DISCUSSION

Watch the video for session one. If you find it helpful, use the following space to take a few notes on anything that stands out to you.

Teaching Notes

DISCUSSION QUESTIONS

After the teaching session has ended, discuss as a group any or all of the following questions.

1. Read **Matthew 17:14–20.** According to this passage, why is prayer the "greatest secret weapon God has given to his people"? What did Jesus say was required on the disciples' part for this prayer to work?

2. Whether playing an instrument, reading a book, cooking, or riding a bicycle—there is a way things work. We know that to get good at something, it takes practice. Why do we tend to have a different attitude when it comes to prayer?

3. Read **Luke 11:1–4.** What are some aspects of Jesus' prayer life that motivated his disciples to want the same? Why did Jesus give them this prayer as a model to follow?

4. Think about the story in the video of the wildfire, which burned 20,000 acres and consumed more than 340 homes in Colorado Springs. What does this story reveal about the power of prayer? What questions does it raise about how prayer works?

5. Read **Ephesians 4:11–16.** In what ways does Paul say that God is "growing us up"? How does God use prayer to help us mature in Christ?

6. Read **1 Kings 18:41–45.** What does this story reveal about being persistent in prayer? What do you tend to do when you don't see any results from your prayers?

7. In **James 5:17**, we read, "Elijah was a human being, even as we are." What is James saying about the power we have been given in prayer? Do you believe you have access to this same power?

PRAYER EXERCISE

Okay—this may prove to be the best part of your work in this study guide. I want you to pick a "prayer project" that you can begin to "practice" on. Like anything else in life—music, driving, sports, love—we learn as we practice, and as we practice we get better. So, pick something that you want to see changed through the power of prayer, and begin to make it a daily practice to pray into it, applying the things you are learning in this book and video series.

Caution: DO NOT pick something massive for this "exercise." What I mean is, some prayer projects are harder than others and very difficult projects would fall into the realm of things like, "my husband's salvation," or, "healing my friend of breast cancer," or "ending global terrorism." Those are all *very* worthy things to pray about; but things like this also fall into the category of "grad school prayer," prayer that is probably going to take time and effort.

For this exercise, pick something small like that presentation you need to make at school or work next week, or the conversation you want to have with your friend on a touchy subject. Things that fall within the realm of, "I can pray about that every day, and if I do I will probably see some results in the near future."

Write down one, two, or three prayer "projects" here. Also write out your prayer for each as well. We'll check in next time to see how things are going.

Note

1. Francis Thompson, *The Hound of Heaven* (Harrisburg, Pa.: Morehouse, 1992), 24.

THE CRY OF
THE HEART

The Father loves you like he loves Jesus. Is this in your mind and heart as you come to prayer? You are not an orphan. You are not merely a "servant" of God. You are a son or daughter. And with that comes privileges: "But when the time had fully come, God sent his Son, born of a woman, born under law, to redeem those under law, that we might receive the full rights of sons" (Galatians 4:4–5).

J O H N   E L D R E D G E

PERSONAL PREPARATION

This week, read chapters 3 and 4 in *Moving Mountains:* "The Cry of the Heart" and "Who He Is and Who We Are." Let's begin again simply with your reaction to the chapters. What did this content stir in you?

The Cry of the Heart

» At the beginning of chapter 3, I write that some prayers just happen—they are "the Cry of the Heart." We don't need any kind of training when it comes to this kind of prayer.

> I've uttered it thousands of times; I'm confident you have too. Like when the phone rings and the bad news starts to spill and all you can do is say, *Father. . . Father. . . Father*, your heart crying out to God. It's a beautiful expression of prayer, rising from the deep places in us, often unbidden, always welcome to his loving ears. The Psalms are filled with this emotive praying:
>
> > I cried out to God for help;
> > > I cried out to God to hear me.
> > > When I was in distress, I sought the Lord (77:1–2).
>
> > Hear my cry, O God;
> > > listen to my prayer.

From the ends of the earth I call to you,
  I call as my heart grows faint;
  lead me to the rock that is higher than I.
For you have been my refuge,
  a strong tower against the foe (61:1–3).

How long, O LORD? Will you forget me forever?
  How long will you hide your face from me?
How long must I wrestle with my thoughts
  and every day have sorrow in my heart?
How long will my enemy triumph over me? (13:1–2).

Doesn't something within you resonate simply reading those words of the psalmist? Our soul responds, *Yes*. There is a kinship here. Words are being put to places we have known. Words like "distress" and "my heart grows faint" and "refuge" play like a bowstring on the cello of our hearts. As does, "how long?" I let go a deep sigh I didn't even know was there; I didn't know I was holding my breath in that way. "How long?" is a phrase you run into many places in the Psalms; it is so true to the human condition (*Moving Mountains*, pages 26–27).

In what ways does your heart resonate with these psalms? How can you hear your heart's cry in them?

The Cry of the Heart just comes, if you'll let it. These are the prayers I find myself already praying as I'm waking up in the morning. "O God—help. Help me today, Lord." Sometimes it's just one word, repeated in my heart: *Jesus, Jesus, Jesus*. I think it will just flow for you, too, if you give it permission. Turn the editor off; let your heart and soul speak (page 27).

» Are you familiar with this kind of praying—spontaneous, informal, anytime anywhere? When do you find yourself saying these kinds of prayers?

[David] certainly isn't embarrassed by the world reading his journals; nothing is hidden here. David quite lustily sails the seven seas of human emotion in his prayers. . . . These psalms are given to the church as our prayer book, our primer, and they are beautiful. Assuring us that not only can God handle the full span of our emotional life, he *invites us* to bring it to him. . . . I find myself embarrassed by how "formal" my prayer life has become, how careful. As I read the Psalms and watch Jesus pray, I realize I am not allowing my heart's full range of emotion to express itself in my prayers, as if I had to somehow shield God from the full depth of the seas within me (pages 30–31).

» Do your prayers sound like David's and the other psalmists'? Do you feel assured that God can handle the full range of your emotions? Why or why not?

The Cry of the Heart is not something you have to arrange for, or practice, or even learn. It doesn't require religious language. You do not have to kneel or close your eyes (and a good thing, too, because most of my praying takes place in the car or as I'm out walking in the woods). There needs to be nothing formal about it at all; in fact, do everything you possibly can to get rid of all formality, all those "thees" and "thous" and religious posturing. Just give it permission. Those prayers are in there (page 33).

» What would it look like to "give yourself permission" for praying this way?

Who He Is and Who We Are

» In chapter 4, I write about a dear friend who is currently in a heinous battle with cancer. My friend has waged this battle for years now, and I do not know if we are in the final hours or not.

Only God knows the number of prayers that have gone up for him; it feels like the number of stars in the heavens. This morning we received a turn of bad news and immediately went to prayer. But I did not feel confident and assured; I certainly did not feel triumphant. I wasn't expecting a cloud the size of a man's fist rising from the sea. I felt discouraged and distressed—my gaze was fixed on his suffering, not upon the resources of the living God (pages 36–37).

Can you relate? What are you typically "looking at" (focused on) as you pray—God or the problem at hand? Explain.

The "wallpaper" on my computer—the background image that fills the entire screen—is a gorgeous photo of a piece of ocean and rugged coastline in Ireland. Our family spent an idyllic summer holiday there. One look at this photo and I am reminded of everything I know to be true about God: *he is the creator of everything I love.* Waterfalls, mountains, wild places; rivers, forests, sunshine, the night sky; beauty, goodness, truth. Just start there—think of all the things you love in this world. And then remind yourself that the God you are praying to is the one who made them all (page 40).

» This is a wonderful exercise: start naming all the things you love in this world. List them below. Then look at them and "remind yourself that the God you are praying to is the one who made them all."

Now get this—there are roughly one hundred billion stars of all sizes in a galaxy, and one hundred billion galaxies in the universe. Which means there are approximately four hundred billion billion suns like ours that God has made. If you began counting to that number today, you could not finish the task in your lifetime. Meanwhile, God is providing the energy of those suns every moment. J.B. Phillips nailed the predicament of too many Christians: "Your God is too small."[1] Words seem ridiculous at this point, but let us say clearly: Power is not an issue with God. His resources are unlimited. Is this the Person you have in mind as you pray? (page 42).

» Who are you praying to? Is he adequate? Is he kind? Is he in a good mood? Where is he located? Is he near or far away?

» How does this help you realize the way you have been thinking of God as you pray?

> A slave feels reluctant to pray; they feel they have no right to ask, and so their prayers are modest and respectful. They spend more time asking forgiveness than they do praying for abundance. They view the relationship with reverence, maybe more like fear, but not with the tenderness of love. Of *being* loved. There is no intimacy in the language or their feelings. Sanctified unworthiness colors their view of prayer. These are often "good servants of the Lord." An orphan is not reluctant to pray; they feel desperate. But their prayers feel more like begging than anything else. Orphans feel a great chasm between themselves and the One to whom they speak. Abundance is a foreign concept; a poverty mentality permeates their prayer life. They ask for scraps; they expect scraps. But not sons; sons know who they are (page 49).

» Do your prayers sound like those of the orphan, the slave, or a son or daughter? Explain.

Dallas Willard said that we ought to look at our lives with God as a partnership. Not as needy, coming to the Lord of the universe hoping for some help, but as partners in a shared mission. This is how Jesus wanted us to see it: "Greater love has no one than this, that he lay down his life for his friends. You are my friends if you do what I command. I no longer call you servants, because a servant does not know his master's business. Instead, I have called you friends, for everything that I learned from my Father I have made known to you" (John 15:13–15). Not only a son or daughter, you are also a friend of God—his confidant, his ally in bringing about his work on this earth (page 53).

» How would this change the way you pray if you allowed it to be true for you?

THE BIG IDEAS

» God assures us in his Word that he can handle the full span of our emotions—and that he wants us to bring those emotions to him.

» The Cry of the Heart removes the formalities we have set in prayer and allows us to connect with God on a deeper level.

» When we pray, we do not come to God as orphans or slaves but as his children. God loves to bless us, his children, when we make our needs known to him.

GROUP DISCUSSION

Watch the video for session two. If you find it helpful, use the following space to take a few notes on anything that stands out to you.

Teaching Notes

DISCUSSION QUESTIONS

After the teaching session has ended, discuss as a group any or all of the following questions.

1. Read **Psalm 77:1–2, 61:1–2** and **13:1–2**. What range of emotions do the psalmists express in these verses? Do you feel comfortable sharing similar emotions with God in your prayers?

2. Read **Psalm 62:8**. What does this verse reveal to us about how God wants us to pray?

3. How did Jesus pray on the night he was betrayed (see **Matthew 26:38–39; Mark 14:34–25; Luke 22:44**)? What does his example show us about being open and honest with God?

4. How often do you, like Jesus, offer up "prayers and petitions with loud cries and tears" (**Hebrews 5:7**)? What do you feel holds you back from doing this more frequently?

5. Read **Luke 15:18–19**. How did the prodigal son believe his father viewed him? How is this reflected in the speech he planned to say to him?

6. Read **Luke 15:20–23**. How does the father's response reveal to us the way God views us? How should knowing we are sons and daughters of God affect our prayers?

PRAYER EXERCISE

Let's check in on the prayer projects you wrote down in session one—how are things going? Are you praying about these daily? If not, what seems to be getting in the way?

What progress are you seeing on any of the projects you are praying into? What are you learning?

This week, while you keep at it on your "projects," I want to encourage you to add the Cry of the Heart to your prayer life. Meaning, when you are in the car, at home, going to bed or rising in the morning, just let your heart express itself to God. Nothing formal, no "projects" here—just allow your heart to cry out to God with whatever is in there.

Note

1. J.B. Phillips, *Your God Is Too Small* (New York: Simon and Schuster, 2004).

SESSION 3

THE PRAYER OF INTERVENTION

We really thought this life was simply about getting a nice little situation going for ourselves and living out the length of our days in happiness. I'm sorry to take that from you, but you and I shall soon be inheriting kingdoms, and we are almost illiterate when it comes to ruling. So God must prepare us to reign. How does he do this? In exactly the same way he grows us up—he puts us in situations that require us to pray and to learn how to use the authority that has been given to us. How else could it possibly happen?

JOHN ELDREDGE

PERSONAL PREPARATION

This week, read chapters 5 and 6 in *Moving Mountains:* "Bold Authority" and "The Prayer of Intervention." Let's begin again simply with your reaction to the chapters. What did this content stir in you?

Bold Authority

» The big idea in chapter 5 is simply this: *You have been given the authority of Jesus to use in prayer.* As you think about your history with prayer, how has the idea of "authority" played a role in your prayer life?

Wisdom is largely cultivated on encountering the laws of the physical world and adjusting our lives to accommodate. Better still, we learn to use those laws to our advantage—we cook with that heat, we build with that lumber. The same holds true in the spiritual realm—there is a way things work. Like the children in a fairy tale, we have been thrust into a collision of *kingdoms.* Kingdoms are realms that are governed by a ruler (the king) and they operate on the basis of *authority.* Back in the story of Daniel and his three-week fast, the angel finally shows up and explains he would have been there sooner but he was blocked by the territorial spirit that held sway over the Persian kingdom. He eventually got through, but did you notice how? He brought in a higher-ranking angel: "The prince of the

Persian kingdom resisted me twenty-one days. Then Michael, one of the chief princes, came to help me, because I was detained there with the king of Persia. Now I have come . . ." (Daniel 10:13–14). The messenger got through the blockade because the mighty archangel Michael came and used his greater authority (and no doubt power). That is what we are doing when we use Jesus' name—we are using his authority (*Moving Mountains*, page 59).

» Is this what you understood yourself to be doing when you used Jesus' name in prayer? In what ways might this perspective add more authority to your prayers?

"Yes . . ." you might say. "I believe Jesus won. So why don't prayers work better than they do? Isn't Satan defeated?" Stay with me now, because this has staggering implications for you and the way you pray. The invasion of the kingdom of God *is something that is still unfolding*, right now, today. Jesus is not merely seated upon a throne somewhere up in the sky:

Christ has indeed been raised from the dead, the firstfruits of those who have fallen asleep. For since death came through a man, the resurrection of the dead comes also through a man. . . . Then the end will come, when he hands over the kingdom to God the Father after he has destroyed all dominion, authority and power. *For he must reign until* he has put all his enemies under his feet (1 Corinthians 15:20–25, emphasis added).

That "until" gives us a very different way of under-standing how Jesus is reigning at the current moment (and why world events still seem so chaotic). Are all his enemies under his feet? Clearly not; the verse says not, and the evening news illustrates it. Jesus, Son of God, Lord of angel armies, is "reigning *until*" he has finished what he began. The image that comes to mind is the ter-rible battle for the South Pacific in World War II. Island by island, bunker by bunker, tunnel by tunnel, a bloody battle had to be waged until the enemy was thoroughly and completely rooted out. Yes—we took the beach at Iwo Jima, and the airstrip. The enemy was defeated, but still he fought on; subduing the entire island was an unspeak-ably savage undertaking (page 62).

» How would the idea that Jesus is currently reigning until he brings all things into submission change the way you approach prayer?

God placed all things under the feet of Jesus and appoint-ed him to be head of everything for *who*? For the church—for you and me. And then, to make it perfectly clear, our Father seats us with Christ right there in authority, at his right hand:

> But because of his great love for us, God, who is rich in mercy, made us alive with Christ even when we were dead in transgressions—it is by grace you have been saved. And God raised us up with

Christ and seated us with him in the heavenly realms in Christ Jesus (Ephesians 2:4–6).

Talk about lavish and scandalous—you have been given a share in the authority of Jesus Christ, Son of the living God, Lord of the heavens and the earth. Do you wield it in prayer? Can you see that it just might make a difference if you did? (pages 68–69).

» Do you wield Jesus' authority in prayer? Can you see it would make a difference if you did? Or do you approach prayer only asking God to do things *for* you? Explain.

The Prayer of Intervention

» The events depicted in Acts 12:1-7, about the early church praying fervently for Peter's release from prison, is told in such realistic detail that it must be for our benefit.

First, notice how the fates of James and Peter are set in contrast, one against the other, in one narrative flow. The story of James's execution is reported in one sentence—quickly, abruptly, like the event itself, like the swift fall of the sword that took his life. A few words, and it is over; it is so abrupt it is almost violent, as was what happened. Peter's story takes longer to tell, because Peter's story is a story of rescue. The next thing we notice is that Peter's deliverance appears connected to verse 5: "the church prayed very earnestly for him." Scripture includes and omits things for a reason. James seems to have been seized and executed rather suddenly; the church is not reported to have been praying for him. Were they caught off guard? Then Peter is seized, and the church is reported to be praying earnestly, and his outcome is different. Whatever you want to make of the contrast (they are contrasted with each other), Peter's story clearly illustrates the Prayer of Intervention (page 75).

What do you make of the story of Peter's rescue? How have you been part of prayer vigils like the one described here?

Clearly, God does not just zap Peter out of prison. The church has to pray "strenuously" for him; the event goes on into the night. He does not zap the promised rain either—Elijah had to climb to the top of the mountain, and there he prayed eight rounds of intervening prayer. God did send the angel to Daniel the first day he prayed—but it took *three weeks* for him to break through. God didn't just zap Joseph, Mary, and the child Jesus down into safety in Egypt—an angel had to come to them as well; they had to flee in the night (page 78).

» How do these stories change the way you view the way God works in the world?

An old saint who first taught me to pray—may he be blessed forever—would often say, "When you think you are finished praying, you are probably just getting warmed up." Often when we first turn to prayer, we are coming in out of the Matrix—that whirling, suffocating Mardi Gras of this world— and it takes us some time to calm down and turn our gaze to Jesus, *fix* our gaze on him. We begin to tune in and align ourselves with God as his partners. That itself takes some time. Much of the early stages of our praying involves not so much interceding but getting ourselves back into align- ment with God and his kingdom. Once in that place, we can begin to be aware of what the Spirit is leading us to pray. Furthermore, as we "press into" prayer, we are not simply begging God to move, but partnering with him in bringing his kingdom to bear on the need at hand. Enforcing that kingdom often requires much "staying with it," and repeti- tion (pages 81–82).

» These are big ideas. In what ways are they giving you a new out- look on how prayer works?

Now we can come back to the wildfire, the angel, and the prayers that saved our home. . . . I personally know many of the men and women who were praying for us. Like the crowd gathered at Mary's home, they are people who are trained in the ways of the kingdom; these men and women . . .

- know who they are in the kingdom of God—not orphans, nor slaves, but sons and daughters of the King, his friends and allies;
- believe that intervening prayer is more than just asking God to do something;

- understand authority—and the authority they have been given, and they are bold enough to use it;
- choose to unite with others in prayer in order to increase their effectiveness; and
- accept the truth that the authority they have been given extends over creation (pages 87–88).

» Look over these five points. Is there anything keeping you from accepting these truths for yourself? How might this change the way you pray this week?

THE BIG IDEAS

» We have been given the authority of Jesus to use in prayer.
» We come to the Lord of the universe not needy and hoping for some help, but as partners in a shared mission.
» Intervening prayer often takes time, and it takes *repetition,* as we repeatedly invoke the authority of Christ over the situation.

GROUP DISCUSSION

Watch the video for session three. If you find it helpful, use the following space to take a few notes on anything that stands out to you.

Teaching Notes

DISCUSSION QUESTIONS

After the teaching session has ended, discuss as a group any or all of the following questions.

1. Read **Matthew 8:5–10.** What did the centurion say that "astonished" Jesus? What did the centurion understand about "the way things work" in the spiritual realm?

2. God made the earth and gave Adam and Eve the authority to rule over it. Yet because of their disobedience, "the whole world lies under the power of the evil one" (**1 John 5:19**). According to **Colossians 2:13–15** and **Philippians 2:9–10**, how did Jesus win it back? What authority does Jesus now hold in our world?

3. Read **Matthew 28:18.** What does it mean when we pray in Jesus' name? How can this understanding of Jesus' authority affect our prayers for God to intervene in situations?

4. Read **Acts 12:5-11**. These events take place shortly after King Herod had James arrested and Peter thrown into prison. What does this passage tell us about the way in which the early church members prayed for Peter? What does it tell us about the way they viewed the power of prayer?

5. Why didn't God just "zap" Peter out of prison? Why do you think God wants us to be persistent and earnest when we seek him through prayers of intervention?

6. In the wildfire story, you saw a demonstration of how to (1) proclaim the truth, (2) invoke the authority of Jesus, and (3) enforce his kingdom over the situation. In what ways is this similar or different from the ways we typically pray? How is prayer *active* rather than *passive*?

PRAYER EXERCISE

Now we are going to "take things up a notch." We have before us a new way of praying—the Prayer of Intervention. Practice this on your current "prayer projects," the ones you wrote down in session one. (And if by now those projects have been answered, or the event has passed, then take time to write down a few new ones!)

In fact, you can even take the prayer I wrote out in the chapter—the one illustrating what the saints might have been praying the night Peter was rescued—and use it yourself. Put the name of the person or the issue you are praying for in place of Peter's name. It's not a perfect fit, but God can sort that out; it will certainly give you a guideline by which to practice "intervening" prayer!

THE PRAYER OF CONSECRATION

In our eagerness to see good happen, Christians often jump straight
into praying, without first pausing and aligning ourselves with Jesus—
like a trombone player who simply starts playing her part without
waiting for the conductor; or an athlete who skips all his normal
stretches and warm-ups and tries to hurl himself into the game
from a cold start. This might be the number one error made
by earnest folk. Remember—there is a way things work. We are in a
collision of kingdoms, and it takes intentionality to bring things
under and into the kingdom of God.

J O H N   E L D R E D G E

PERSONAL PREPARATION

This week, read chapters 7 and 8 in *Moving Mountains:* "Removing One More Obstacle" and "Consecration—Bringing Things Under the Rule of Jesus." Begin with your reaction to the chapters. What did this material arouse in you?

Removing One More Obstacle

» In chapter 7, I try to untangle a few impediments to prayer that have worked their way into our theology—though they are not contained in Scripture. One of these is that "prayer moves the hand of God."

> Follow the logic. Prayer moves the hand of God—in other words, God is waiting to move until I pray. That thought alone reflects such a debased view of God I give thanks it is false, foul heresy. The entire story of God toward us begins with God making the first move: "In the beginning God . . ." (Genesis 1:1). That theme carries on throughout the Bible:
>
>> You see, at just the right time, when we were still powerless, Christ died for the ungodly. . . . God demonstrates his own love for us in this: While we were still sinners, Christ died for us (Romans 5:6, 8).
>>
>> You did not choose me, but I chose you (John 15:16).
>>
>> No one can come to me unless the Father who sent me draws him (John 6:44).

In the same way, the Spirit helps us in our weak-
ness. We do not know what we ought to pray for,
but the Spirit himself intercedes for us with groans
that words cannot express (Romans 8:26).

The tender, beautiful revelation in the parable of the
lost son is that the father could not have seen his son coming from "a long ways off" unless *he* was first looking for his
son (*Moving Mountains*, pages 90–91).

Are you able to see how "prayer moves the hand of God" is not
what the Bible teaches—especially when you apply it to any earth-
ly father? How has this changed your perception of prayer?

» God moves first—in your life. What does this truth do for your
heart and soul?

"And the Lord said, 'Listen to what the unjust judge says.
And will not God bring about justice for his chosen ones,
who cry out to him day and night? Will he keep putting them off? I tell you, he will see that they get justice,
and quickly'" (Luke 18:6–8). Surely you understand that
Jesus was *not* characterizing God like that judge. God is
not someone you have to beg and beg in order to irritate
enough to move his hand. Jesus says so at the end of the

lesson. He taught us to call upon him as Father, Abba, Papa. The story is introduced as "a parable to show them that they should always pray and not give up." It is about *persistence*. It is about the Prayer of Intervention (pages 93–94).

» How might this help you with long prayer projects that seem to see no results?

Consecration—Bringing Things Under the Rule of Jesus

» Chapter 8 is devoted to the idea of consecration—intentionally bringing things under and into the kingdom of God.

In teaching healing prayer, Agnes Sanford used this wonderfully simple analogy:

> If we try turning on an electric iron and it does not work, we look to the wiring of the iron, the cord, or the house. We do not stand in dismay before the iron and cry, "Oh, electricity, *please* come into my iron and make it work!" We realize that while the whole world is full of that mysterious power we call electricity, only the amount that flows through the wiring of the iron will make the iron work for us.[1]

The act of consecration is "repairing the wiring," the first step before God's protection and provision can flow. It is the fresh act of dedicating yourself—or your home, a relationship, a job, your sexuality, whatever needs God's grace—deliberately and intentionally to Jesus, bringing it fully into his kingdom and under his rule. It seems so obvious, now that we state it, but you would be surprised how often this vital step is overlooked (and then folks wonder why their prayers don't seem to be effective) (pages 97–98).

In what ways is this clarifying for you? How might it help your prayers?

Last week Stasi and I were helping some friends consecrate their new home—which is a *very* good idea and something that requires focused intention to do well. . . . The house in question was about thirty years old. They had been living in it for six months when my friend called to say, "Okay, what is going on? The kids are having nightmares, my wife is having headaches, we're fighting all the time. What is this?" My first question was, "Do you know who you bought the house from?" "Not really. It's this older lady." "You have no idea what went on in that house?" "No, no idea." "It would probably be a good idea to bring the kingdom of God there. It was under someone else's dominion for a long time and you have no idea what they let in. All it takes is their kids listening to heavy metal and that provides a huge invitation for foul spirits to come in and hang out there. You don't know what kind of music their kids listened to, what movies they watched, what their religious beliefs were; you don't know what went on in that house"[2] (pages 97, 105).

» Have you consecrated your home, or apartment, bedroom, living space? If not, what kept you from doing so? If you have, how long ago was it—and was it as thorough as described here?

Think of consecration as "aligning" and "enforcing"—*aligning* yourself, or the subject in question, with Jesus and all the laws of his kingdom, then *enforcing* his rule and those laws over the matter in question. The first steps, which we have covered already, are mostly the aligning part. But often the enforcing requires a bit more oomph, especially if you are having difficulties there. Which brings me to the power of *proclaiming*. . . . We enforce by proclaiming what is true over the subject at hand. For example, we proclaim our authority over our homes because we do have that authority, and we are requiring all things in the heavens and the earth to recognize and yield to that authority. We are announcing to all kingdoms and powers that the authority of Jesus Christ is now in effect *here*. Proclaiming also causes your own spirit to rise up—or the spirit of the person you are praying for. Everything sort of stands at attention when you begin to proclaim the truth (pages 109–110).

» How does "aligning" and "enforcing" fit in with your growing understanding of your authority in Jesus, the collision of kingdoms in this world, and the importance of bringing things back under the rule of Jesus?

» In what ways can you now see this is different than just asking God to do it?

THE BIG IDEAS

» Prayer does not move the hand of God—the entire story we find in Scripture of God toward us begins with him making the first move.

» The act of consecration is the first step we must take for God's protection and provision to flow into our lives.

» Consecration is aligning ourselves with Jesus, enforcing his rule, and proclaiming what is true over the situation at hand.

GROUP DISCUSSION

Watch the video for session four. If you find it helpful, use the following space to take a few notes on anything that stands out to you.

Teaching Notes

DISCUSSION QUESTIONS

After the teaching session has ended, discuss as a group any or all of the following questions.

1. Read **Exodus 19:10–11** and **Joshua 3:5**. Why did God give these instructions to the Isralietes? Why was consecration necessary for what he was about to do in their midst?

2. Read **Acts 13:1–4**. What was involved in Barnabas and Paul consecrating themselves before the Lord? What was the result?

3. Read **Daniel 10:12–13**. Why was the answer to Daniel's prayer delayed? What does this reveal about the spiritual forces at work in our world?

4. How does the prayer of consecration bring us back under the rule of Jesus so we can experience his blessings?

5. Read **Romans 6:13** and **12:1**. What does it mean to "offer ourselves" to God? How does this enable God's healing and blessings to flow into our lives?

6. Why is it important to not only consecrate ourselves but also our home, office, travel, possessions, and relationships?

7. What is the purpose in beginning our day with consecrating prayer? What are we committing to God when we do this?

PRAYER EXERCISE

Time to consecrate! In the space below, list some things in your world that you now see you would like to consecrate and bring under the rule of Jesus.

Now take the things you have listed above and pray through each one slowly and carefully, consecrating it to Jesus Christ and his kingdom! If you are consecrating your home/apartment/bedroom, use the prayer I included in the chapter (see pages 105–106); it also helps to pray the prayer while you are in that particular space. The same holds true for your work—if you can (perhaps quietly), do the act of consecration in your office/cubicle/space. If it is your sexuality you want to consecrate, use the longer prayer offered in the back of the book (see pages 239–243); it will prove much more effective. For all other things, you can use the prayer of consecration for a home and adapt it to whatever it is you are consecrating . . .

> *Father, thank you for the blessing and the provision of this [name the object]. I (or we) bring it under my authority now, and under the authority of Jesus Christ. I take full authority over this [object], in the name of Jesus Christ. I take a total and complete authority over this entire [object] now, in Jesus' name. I renounce all ungodliness and all sinful activity that has ever taken place regarding this [object]. I renounce the sins of all previous owners, users, etc. I cancel every claim the enemy can make here, by the blood of Jesus Christ. I cleanse this [object] with the blood of Christ—everything spiritual, everything physical. I consecrate and dedicate this [object] to the rule of Jesus Christ, and to the Holy Spirit. Come, Holy Spirit, come and fill every part of this [object] with the glory of your kingdom, with love, with peace, [and the blessings you want to see here]. Jesus, I ask your angels to cleanse this [object] now, to establish your kingdom here, to build a shield of protection around it. In the mighty name of Jesus Christ the Lord, I now proclaim this [object] the property of the kingdom of God.*

Notes

1. Agnes Sanford, *The Healing Light* (New York: Ballantine, 1972), 1.
2. Sin is typically the reason things get out from under the protection and provision of God. It was Adam and Eve's sin that gave the evil one dominion over us and over this earth; what followed was the suffering and brokenness that has become our daily reality. That suffering and brokenness is what we are trying to fix through prayer. Therefore our first aim ought to be getting things back under the dominion of God and the provision of his kingdom.

BONUS INSERT

DAILY PRAYER
AND PRAY NOW!

I don't know how many Christian meetings I've been in—board meetings, elder meetings—when all the time is used talking about what needs prayer, and we find we have barely a few minutes left at the end for one quick, little, rushed prayer. It's a brilliant ploy of the enemy—keep God's people talking about it, debating, conjecturing, worrying over it, speculating, so they never really get around to praying. By all means, pray when you have time and space to devote yourself to it, time to truly seek God. But pray now too—because you don't know that you will get to it later.

J O H N   E L D R E D G E

PERSONAL PREPARATION

Let me explain this "bonus" content. Due to limiting factors, we chose not to cover chapter 9, "Daily Prayer," and chapter 10, "Pray Now!" in the videos. But I believe they are certainly worth your time if you are going through the book. So, if you are *only* watching the videos, you can skip this study. Here we will process the ideas covered in chapters 9 and 10 from the book. Begin with your reaction to the chapters. What did this content arouse in you?

Pray Now!

» Let's actually start with the simple idea in chapter 10—we need to pray now, or we might not ever get to it!

> I've come to the place where I have had to stop telling people, "I'll pray for you." I simply know that despite my good intentions—and these promises are almost always spoken with good intent—I know that nine times out of ten I just don't remember to follow through. Not until maybe a week or two later, and then I feel guilty that I forgot. I don't like promising something I probably won't live up to. You know how these stories go: Someone you care about tells you of their pain, need, or struggle, and you respond with, "Oh, I'm so sorry to hear that; I'll pray for you." But then, most of the time, we never do (*Moving Mountains*, page 122).

Can you relate? When have you found this to be true for you?

» This is a good point to stop and do some evaluation. What are the things that typically get in the way of your praying?

» What can you practically do to address those hindrances? Can you "pray now" by praying when you drive, or exercise, or while taking your lunch break?

Daily Prayer

» In this chapter, I write about the importance of having a daily time of prayer with God.

> Now that you have some understanding of the collision of the kingdoms going on all around you, and the need to be intentional about "remaining" in daily intimacy and union with Jesus, I think you have a better grasp of why some sort of daily prayer is essential. Not a quick little, "Father, help me today" prayer; not even interceding for others. Not as your first move. What we need first is *aligning* prayer—bringing ourselves fully back into alignment with Jesus, taking our place in him and his kingdom, drawing upon his life and the power of his work for us. Over the past thirty years I have progressed from one form of daily prayer to

another. I think you will see something of the progression from children to young men to fathers in the development of my morning prayers (page 112).

Do you currently practice some sort of daily prayer? Can you see your own progression over the years from "children" to "young men (and women)" to "fathers (and mothers)"? How have your prayers matured over time?

» How are your prayers maturing as you do this study?

Now, before you jump in, let me offer another piece of advice an old saint gave me years ago when I was just learning to pray. He told me, "Whenever I realize that I have lost paying attention and switched to just 'saying words,' I go back, and pick it up from there." That one act has proven massively helpful in learning effective prayer. This is not mindless rep- etition; we must be utterly *present* to it. Remember what E.M. Bounds said: "The entire man must pray. The whole man—life, heart, temper, mind, are all in it . . . it takes a whole heart to do effectual praying."[1] There is a need to keep at it—like chipping away at ice (page 114).

» Do you get distracted during prayer? If so, how would "going back" and picking it up from where you lost focus be a help to you?

I will often repeat words and phrases as I go along, adding further intentionality. When I say "I surrender every aspect and dimension of my life to you," I will often add, "utterly, utterly, utterly." For we wander, and we have often given ourselves over to other things, and coming home to God therefore requires some time and focus (page 115).

» Do you allow yourself to repeat parts of your prayers, or pause and add emphasis? What is the value in doing so?

Next, we begin to relate to each member of the Trinity. God is Father, Son, and Holy Spirit—and you have a relationship with each one in unique ways. You need certain things from the Father, from Jesus, and from the Holy Spirit. This is part of our growing up—not just a generic prayer to God but relating to the Trinity as mature allies relate to one another (page 116).

» In what ways have you allowed yourself to have a relationship with each member of the Trinity? Is the idea exciting to you? Why or why not?

As I shift to Jesus, I pray intentionally into the cross, the resurrection, and the ascension. God the Father has provided everything you need for your restoration in the work of Christ. So many people wonder why God doesn't come through for them more, when they have not even begun to take advantage of and enforce the massive things he *already* provided. Your Father included you in each element of the work of Christ (all of it was for you, after all; Jesus didn't need these things; you did). Taking our place in, and receiving the fullness of, his work is vital (pages 116–117).

» This is a really big idea—that God our Father *has* intervened on our behalf, far more than we know, and we cannot begin to assess our place in this world until we first take advantage of the full work of Christ on a daily basis. What does that idea do for you?

I have been embracing and entering into the work of Christ in a fresh way; now I begin to enforce it over my life and kingdom. (The entire prayer is "proclaiming, invoking, and enforcing") (page 118).

» Do you enforce the full work of Christ over your life and "kingdom" on a regular basis? If not, what might begin to change if you did?

Then I will cleanse myself once more and put on the full armor of God. A word on this—the armor of God is not a metaphor. I think most people have a vague notion about it, not realizing that the armor is a real thing. You are actually putting on real combat gear in the spirit realm; it is just as real as God, whom you cannot see. Take it seriously; this is not symbolic, but actual equipment provided for your safety (page 120).

» Has the "armor of God" been rather vague to you? Symbolic? Or have you seen it as a real set of actual combat gear? Does the reality of the war we find ourselves in help you to see that it is? Explain.

THE BIG IDEAS

» We need to pray *now*, or we might not ever get to it.
» There is a collision of kingdoms going on all around us, which is why we need to be intentional about remaining in daily intimacy and union with Jesus.
» God *has* intervened on our behalf, and we cannot assess our place in this world until we first take advantage of the full work of Christ on a daily basis.

Prayer Exercise

Before we take on this week's exercise, check in on your prayer projects. Have you been trying the Prayer of Intervention? What seem to be the results?

Now for an important tip—remember in the story of Elijah, how he would "go at it" for a while and then check to see if it was having any effect? This is a practical way to approach prayer. Using the various methods we have talked about, you can go at your prayer project(s) and then see if anything seems to be having a noticeable effect. Does it need consecration? Does "enforcing" the rule of Jesus over it help?

This week's exercise is simple—try the Daily Prayer! It might help you to download the free Ransomed Heart app onto your mobile device. The Daily Prayer is there (along with many others) in both a written and an audio version; the audio allows you to pray right along with me! Give it a try for seven days, and see if you experience the fruits of it!

Note

1. Edward M. Bounds, *The Complete Works of E.M. Bounds on Prayer: Experience the Wonders of God Through Prayer* (Grand Rapids: Baker, 2004), 70.

S E S S I O N 5

LISTENING PRAYER

Jesus—what should I pray in this? will prove revolutionizing to your prayer life. The intimacy you will experience with God will nourish your soul; it is so satisfying you will crave more and more. But your prayers will also be so much more effective. Again, God loves and honors our prayers as children, and as young men and women, but nowadays I rarely pray any other way than from, Jesus—what do I pray?

J O H N E L D R E D G E

PERSONAL PREPARATION

This week, read chapters 11 and 12 in *Moving Mountains:* "'Let There Be Light'—Prayer for Guidance, Understanding, and Revelation" and "Listening Prayer." Begin with your reaction to these chapters. What did this material arouse in you?

Listening Prayer

» Because Listening Prayer plays such an important role in prayer for guidance, I'm going to address the ideas from that chapter first. (I'm assuming you have read both chapters 11 and 12; you are reading both chapters each time, aren't you?)

> The single most significant decision that has changed my prayer life more than any other, the one step that has brought about greater results than all others combined is this (drum roll, please). . . Asking Jesus what I should pray. So simple, and so revolutionizing! Utterly obvious once we consider it, but something we so rarely practice. That is probably one of the side effects of the "prayer is just asking God to do something" view; no doubt it is also more of the negative consequences of the orphan-and-slave mentality. But if prayer is in fact a partnership, then I want to be in alignment with God! For here is his promise to us: "This is the confidence we have in approaching God: that if we ask anything according to his will, he hears us. And if we know that he hears us—whatever we ask—we

know that we have what we asked of him" (1 John 5:14–15)
(*Moving Mountains*, page 138).

Is asking Jesus what to pray a new idea for you? If so, can you begin to see why it is so important, based on 1 John 5:14–15?

Despite all the stunning victories in our past, I never assume I know what the new prayer need before me requires. If someone asks me, "Pray that my mother and my father reconcile," I don't simply start praying that. For one thing, I do not know with any sort of certainty that reconciliation is what God is doing in this moment. It may well be the will of God that her parents reconcile, but it may also be that *first* he wants to address something in their character. God doesn't just put Band-Aids on things; it would be far more like him to first deal with the sin that was poisoning the marriage, and then bring about reconciliation. I want to live and pray like God's intimate ally, so I turn my gaze toward God and ask, *What do you want me to pray for her mother and father? Show me what to pray.* Those prayers are far more effective because they are aligned with his will. They are aligned with what he is doing in the situation at this particular moment (pages 139–140).

» Makes sense, doesn't it? What are you praying about these days that you would love to know God's will on the subject? Have you asked him?

Prayer is not making speeches to God; it is entering into conversational intimacy with him. Father to son or daughter, friend to friend, partner to partner, essential prayer is conversational. It involves a give-and-take. Remember the playful exchange between Ananias and Jesus? "You want me to do *what*?" "Go to this specific house. Place your hands on him." "Wait a second—really?" I understand that prayer speeches are what most of us have seen modeled, but there is a fabulous intimacy and effectiveness available to us as we pause and let God say something in return (page 141).

» React to the very big idea that "prayer is not making speeches to God; it is entering into conversational intimacy with him."

We are *meant* to hear the voice of God. This is one of the lost treasures of Christianity—an intimate, conversational relationship with God is available, and is meant to be normal. . . . I realize that many dear followers of Christ have been taught that God only speaks to his sons and daughters through the Bible. The irony of that theology is this: *that's not what the Bible teaches!* The Scriptures are filled with stories of God speaking to his people—intimately, personally. Adam and Eve spoke with God. As did Abraham, Moses, and Elijah. So did Noah, Gideon, Aaron, Isaiah, Jeremiah, Ananias, and the apostle Paul. On and on the examples go (pages 142–143).

» Did you know that "an intimate, conversational relationship with God is available, and is meant to be normal"? How would you like to grow in your experience of such intimacy?

These are the basic steps [to Listening Prayer]: Start with small and simple questions, yes or no questions if possible. Quiet yourself; pull away if you can to a quiet place and shut out all other distractions. Repeat the question as you pray and listen—that helps dial you in and keeps you focused. Bring your heart into a place of surrender (page 147).

» There is a way things work! Write out for yourself the four "steps" toward Listening Prayer I have summarized here.

I don't want to just jump in and start whacking away, only to find myself exhausted thirty minutes later with little to show for it. That can be so discouraging. First, I consecrate and ask the Holy Spirit to fill me. But I don't even start praying after that; second, I ask the Spirit what to pray. How he reveals this is as diverse and creative as the God who made the world around us. Sometimes I will simply hear a word, like, Comfort. So I will begin to pray for comfort. Sometimes he will bring a scripture to mind, and I will let that be the focus of my prayers. Other times he will reveal something key by a "feeling" or a sensation—I will suddenly feel overwhelmed, or discouraged, or fearful when I wasn't moments before—and in that manner he reveals to me what the person I am praying for is under. But most of the time, he will speak to me in my heart—that "small, inner voice"—and give me direction as to what to pray. The more accustomed you become to this approach, the more the Spirit can guide your prayers in the moment, as you pray. It becomes one beautiful, intimate partnership of prayer (page 149).

» It is important to know that God will speak to us in many ways. I name four here; can you name others you recall from stories in the Scripture or experiences you have had?

"Let There Be Light"—Prayer for Guidance, Understanding, and Revelation

» In chapter 11, I introduce the idea of asking for the Spirit of wisdom and revelation.

"For this reason, ever since I heard about your faith in the Lord Jesus and your love for all the saints, I have not stopped giving thanks for you, remembering you in my prayers. I keep asking that the God of our Lord Jesus Christ, the glorious Father, may give you the Spirit of wisdom and revelation, so that you may know him better. I pray also that the eyes of your heart may be enlightened" (Ephesians 1:15–18). When seeking clarity, we will almost always ask for the Spirit of wisdom and revelation. Both are needed. Sometimes, wisdom holds the answer. Other times, we need a revelation from God (as did Ananias, when the situation seemed to shout, "Don't go near Saul!") (page 129).

We need both wisdom and revelation from God. Do you typically lean on one or the other of these? If so, which one, and why?

The key to receiving answers to prayers for guidance is to let go of our constant attempt to "figure things out." Really, it is almost incessant; I will be in the midst of seeking the God of four hundred billion billion suns on some issue of guidance, and in the midst of asking him, I am thinking through the options, trying to figure it out as I pray. I've been in hundreds of meetings where Christians gathered to seek God's counsel on some matter, but they spent the entire time trying to figure it out (pages 129–130).

» Are you personally aware of that constant attempt to figure things out? Why do you suppose we keep trying?

» In this chapter, I summarize four steps to prayer for guidance. Can you name those here? (I'll give you a hint—the first one is "do whatever you can to reduce the pressure.")

THE BIG IDEAS

» Listening Prayer involves asking Jesus what we should pray so we can be in alignment with God's will.
» Prayer is not making speeches to God; it is entering into conversational intimacy with him.
» When seeking clarity, we will almost always ask for the Spirit of wisdom and revelation.

GROUP DISCUSSION

Watch the video for session five. If you find it helpful, use the following space to take a few notes on anything that stands out to you.

Teaching Notes

DISCUSSION QUESTIONS

After the teaching session has ended, discuss as a group any or all of the following questions.

1. Healthy conversations involve a combination of both talking and listening. Why are our prayers to God so often one-sided—with us doing all the talking? What does it mean to truly *listen* to God?

2. Read **1 John 5:14–15**. What promise are we given in this passage? What does this tell us about the ways we should pray and the requests we offer to God?

3. Read **Acts 9:10–12** and **17–18**. How did Ananias act in partnership with God? What was the result of his prayers for Paul?

4. Read **John 10:2–4, 16, and 27**. What did Jesus reveal in this passage about God's desire to communicate with us? Why is it best to "begin small" when learning to hear the voice of God?

5. In **1 Kings 19:12**, we read the voice of the Lord came to Elijah in "a gentle whisper," or a "still, small voice." What are some ways mentioned in the video for us to get rid of distractions so we can hear God's voice?

6. What is the value of repeating a question we ask the Lord in prayer? What does it mean to bring our hearts into a place of surrender to God?

7. How does Listening Prayer change the way we ask God for guidance? How does it change the way we pray for family and friends?

PRAYER EXERCISE

If you are currently in need of guidance, use the prayer for guidance I included in chapter 11 as a tool, inserting your particular question into the model prayer (see pages 133–134). But we also covered Listening Prayer this time around, and it is relevant to everyone all the time, so let's make sure we give that a try! As I wrote:

> The Holy Spirit also empowers our prayers, making them mighty with the power of God. Paul said, "He who unites himself with the Lord is one in spirit with him" (1 Corinthians 6:17), so, whenever I possibly can, I begin every prayer with personal consecration:
>
> > *Jesus—I present myself to you again, right here, right now, in this, for this. I consecrate to you my spirit, soul, and body, my heart, mind, and will. I consecrate to you my gifting, my seeing and perceiving. I consecrate these prayers to you. Wash me with your blood again; cleanse me and renew me. Holy Spirit—come and restore my union with Father and Son; come and fill these prayers* (pages 148–149).

Practice this over the next week: consecrate yourself as I laid out here, and then ask the Spirit of God what to pray. And remember:

> Start with small and simple questions, yes or no questions if possible. Quiet yourself; pull away if you can to a quiet place and shut out all other distractions. Repeat the question as you pray and listen—that helps dial you in and keeps you focused. Bring your heart into a place of surrender (page 147).

One of the best and simplest ways to practice learning to hear the voice of God is to ask Jesus, "Do you love me, Lord?" because you know the answer is yes, based on a thousand scriptures! Listen for that personal "yes."

WARFARE PRAYER

Jesus is actively reigning now until he has completely vanquished the enemy—beach by beach, tunnel by tunnel. And he has clearly called us up into this fight. When Satan was cast down from the heavens, he declared war on the church; that includes you. "Then the dragon was enraged at the woman and went off to make war against. . . those who obey God's commandments and hold to the testimony of Jesus" (Revelation 12:17). We are at war, whether you choose to believe it or not. . . . I believe that part of the reason God has left it to be done this way is because he is growing us up; we too must learn to rule and reign.

JOHN ELDREDGE

PERSONAL PREPARATION

This week, read chapters 13 and 14 in *Moving Mountains:* "Praying Scripture" and "Warfare Prayer." Begin with your reaction to the chapters. What did these truths arouse in you?

Warfare Prayer

» Most of the chapters in the book build upon the previous chapters; this is certainly true with this week's chapters. Because warfare prayer is the topic less familiar to most readers, we will begin there, in chapter 14.

> Now we turn to the form of prayer that often brings the most dramatic and immediate results—prayer that banishes the enemy. It is actually a simple form of prayer, and very effective. The reason more people don't enjoy its wonderful fruits is either because they don't believe we are at war (a worldview that takes massive amounts of denial to sustain) or because they feel intimidated by the subject. So let me make this clear—the enemy *always* tries to keep you from praying against him, as Jesus taught us to pray, because he knows once you learn how to do this, his gig is up. Really—this is extremely simple and yet quite effective (*Moving Mountains*, page 166).

Has warfare prayer been a part of your prayer history? If not, why not? Might it be because you don't believe we are at war or perhaps you feel intimidated by the subject?

The wonderful news is that the cross of Jesus Christ disarmed all foul spirits—the "powers and authorities" (Colossians 2:15), meaning the evil one himself, and all those fallen angels in his armies, like the prince of the Persian kingdom. Having cast them down, all authority was given to Jesus. And then—I suggested that at this point trumpets ought to ring out and banners unfurl—he gave his majestic authority to us: "I have given you authority. . . to overcome all the power of the enemy" (Luke 10:19) (pages 167–168).

» This is SO important that you should write it down right here: "All authority has been given to Jesus. He has given his authority to me."

Notice he doesn't take away the attack; rather, he gives us the authority we need to overcome it. Far better to learn how to shut it down than let it wreak havoc in your kingdom unchecked and unchallenged. You have everything you need to live a life free from Satan's assaults. The demons know your authority in Jesus; they know that if you banish them, they have to obey. Every time they are commanded to in Scripture, they obey. So of course they try to make you feel as though you don't really want to pray like this. They nearly always send distraction, or confusion, all sorts of feelings like, *Really—do we really have to deal with this?* (page 168).

» In fact, I just felt that same "push back" writing this guide: *Don't bother with this; do it tomorrow; do you really want to take this on?* How have you been aware of that attitude working against your prayers?

Resist. Fight back. Take your stand. Scripture is very clear on this point. First, Jesus models it; then the disciples do it, and then Paul and the early church. To make it all perfectly clear, the command to fight is also written down in black and white. This is part of what it means to be a Christian. I am amazed by the hemming and hawing and dodging Christians will go through to avoid this: "It's not your job to resist the devil—that's Jesus' job." No—you have been commanded to resist. "The devil is a toothless lion." No—Scripture says he can steal, kill, and destroy; it says he can devour. "Warfare isn't necessary when we focus on worship; the devil never rushes into the throne room of God." Worship *is* a powerful tool against the enemy. But friends, you do not live in the throne room of God; you live your days here on this earth, in the midst of war, and "your brothers throughout the world are undergoing" spiritual attack (1 Peter 5:9). Including you. . . . I'm curious—why do we accept Jesus as a model for forgiving others, or loving God as Father, or caring for the poor, but not in the simple matter of dealing with the enemy? (pages 168–170).

» Does your theology now have a place for the war and your own personal call to fight? If not, what would it take to convince you?

> For he has rescued us from the dominion of darkness and brought us into the kingdom of the Son he loves, in whom we have redemption, the forgiveness of sins (Colossians 1:13–14).

» What do these verses tell you about your position with the enemy? What has your Father done for you?

> When you were dead in your sins and in the uncircumcision of your sinful nature, God made you alive with Christ. He forgave us all our sins, having canceled the written code, with its regulations, that was against us and that stood opposed to us; he took it away, nailing it to the cross. And having disarmed the powers and authorities, he made a public spectacle of them, triumphing over them by the cross (Colossians 2:13–15).

» Who did your Father and Jesus disarm by the cross?

> Now have come the salvation and the power and the king-
> dom of our God, and the authority of his Christ. For the
> accuser of our brothers. . . has been hurled down. They
> overcame him by the blood of the Lamb and by the word
> of their testimony; they did not love their lives so much as
> to shrink from death (Revelation 12:10–11).

» How do the saints overcome the enemy, according to this passage?

» I laid out four simple steps for effective warfare prayer in the chapter. Write them out here (hint: step one involves identifying the spirit).

> Warfare prayer is not a "backup" category when all else
> fails. It is not a specialty form of prayer for the uniquely
> called or gifted. Yes—there are some who become "experts"
> in this field, just as there are some who become especial-
> ly trained to heal or to preach the gospel. But we are all
> called to preach the gospel; we are all called to resist the
> enemy. You are living out your daily life in the context of
> war. The men and women who choose to equip themselves
> and become practiced in warfare prayer are the ones

who enjoy the greatest freedom and breakthrough—the "glorious freedom of the children of God" (Romans 8:21) (page 184).

» So, where does warfare prayer now fit into your understanding and practice, having read the scriptures and stories included in this chapter? Is it a "backup" form of prayer? A specialized form of prayer for a few? Explain.

Praying Scripture

» The famous model for warfare prayer is the temptation of Christ in the wilderness (see Luke 4). Again and again, Jesus uses Scripture against the enemy, which brings us back to the previous chapter on praying the Word of God. I shared how I take a passage like John 17, and pray through it as I read it:

> I pray for them. I am not praying for the world, but for those you have given me, for they are yours. All I have is yours, and all you have is mine. And glory has come to me through them. I will remain in the world no longer, but they are still in the world, and I am coming to you. Holy Father, protect them by the power of your name—the name you gave me—so that they may be one as we are one. [*Yes, Father, yes—I pray that you would protect me by the power of your name, so that I might be one with you and with Jesus.*]. . . I am coming to you now, but I say these things while I am still in the world, so that they may have the full measure of my joy within them. [*Father, yes—I ask for the*

full measure of the joy Jesus had within me; I ask you for his joy.] I have given them your word and the world has hated them, for they are not of the world any more than I am of the world. My prayer is not that you take them out of the world but that you protect them from the evil one. They are not of the world, even as I am not of it. Sanctify them by the truth; your word is truth. [*Yes, Father, yes—protect me from the evil one; sanctify me by the truth.*] . . . My prayer is not for them alone. I pray also for those who will believe in me through their message, that all of them may be one, Father, just as you are in me and I am in you. May they also be in us so that the world may believe that you have sent me. [*Father, I receive this for my life; I agree in prayer that I might be one with Jesus, and one with you, Father.*] I have given them the glory that you gave me, that they may be one as we are one: I in them and you in me. May they be brought to complete unity to let the world know that you sent me and have loved them even as you have loved me. [*I receive the glory that you gave Jesus, which he has passed on to me, that I may be one with you, Father, just as Jesus is one with you. Jesus in me, and you in Jesus-in-me. May I be brought to complete unity with you, God, so that the world may know you sent Jesus*] (John 17:9–23) (pages 153–154).

Sometimes I will take a passage like this and make it into a prayer built on the scripture:

Father, thank you for giving me to Jesus. I join my prayer with his—I pray that you would protect me from the evil one by the power of your name, the name of Jesus; I pray for the full measure of his joy, which is your joy; I pray you would sanctify me by the truth; I receive the glory that you gave Jesus, which he has passed on to me, that I may be one with you, Father, just as Jesus is one with you. Jesus in me, and you in Jesus-in-me. May I be brought to complete unity with you, God, so that the world may know you sent Jesus (page 155).

» Choose a favorite passage of Scripture, one that you can turn into a prayer right here. Write it out as if it were a prayer to God:

THE BIG IDEAS

» All authority has been given to Jesus, and he has given his authority to us to overcome the attacks of the enemy.
» In the Bible, we are *commanded* to resist and fight back against the attacks of the enemy in whatever form those attacks take.
» When we pray the Scriptures, we have the assurance that we are praying right in the center of God's will.

GROUP DISCUSSION

Watch the video for session six. If you find it helpful, use the following space to take a few notes on anything that stands out to you.

Teaching Notes

DISCUSSION QUESTIONS

After the teaching session has ended, discuss as a group any or all of the following questions.

1. Warfare prayer often has immediate and dramatic results. Read **Acts 16:16–18.** What did Paul do to cause the enemy to leave? How was he able to do this?

2. Read **Ephesians 2:6.** What does this verse say about the authority we have been given in Christ? What images does this passage bring to mind? How would this change our view on prayer if we took this truth to heart?

3. Read **James 4:7** and **1 Peter 5:8–9.** What instructions are we given for how to oppose the work of the enemy? How should these instructions guide our prayers?

4. Read **Luke 10:17–19.** What authority does Jesus give the seventy-two over the enemy? What does this say about our authority?

5. What is the value in naming a specific attack that is taking place against us? Why is it crucial to renounce the enemy's claim against us? What does this involve?

6. Read **Revelation 12:10–11.** How do we bring the work Jesus did for us at the cross against the works of the enemy? What happens when we do this?

7. Why does the enemy try to distract us from praying? How can we recognize these subtle forms of attack and resist them?

PRAYER EXERCISE

The Daily Prayer we examined in chapter 9 is a simple and effective way of doing warfare prayer, because you first take your place in Christ and all his victory and then enforce that victory against your current enemies. If you have been trying the Daily Prayer, keep at it another week. If you haven't, do so now. (As I mentioned in the bonus session, it might help you to download the free Ransomed Heart app onto your mobile device.)

HEALING PRAYER

As we explore the many beautiful and intimate ways Jesus comes to heal our inner beings, keep in mind that whatever the damage may be, in any realm of your inner being, the essence of healing prayer is always to facilitate the presence of Jesus into the specific places of damage. Whatever else might be involved, it always begins with, "Jesus, come into this and heal."

J O H N   E L D R E D G E

PERSONAL PREPARATION

This week, read chapters 15 and 16 in *Moving Mountains:* "Inner Heal-ing—Restoring the Soul" and "Physical Healing." Let me say right at the start here that "understanding" these ideas is not the goal. *Healing your soul* is the goal. You will want to work your way through the healing process very carefully and lovingly, for we have all been wounded and broken in this war. Begin with your reaction to the chapters. What did these truths stir in you?

Inner Healing—Restoring the Soul

» The glorious news is that God restores the soul; he heals the broken heart.

> The LORD is my shepherd. . . .
>   he restores my soul (Psalm 23:1, 3).

> He heals the brokenhearted
>   and binds up their wounds (Psalm 147:3).

> He has sent me to bind up the brokenhearted (Isaiah 61:1).

> When you experience this for yourself, or minister it through prayer to another human being, there is nothing like it on earth. For the search for wholeness compels every person, every hour of their lives, whether they know it or not. We ache to be made whole again (*Moving Mountains*, pages 190–191).

Are you aware of that ache—to be made whole again? Have you pursued healing for your heart and soul? In what way?

The destiny of the human soul is union with God. The same oneness that Jesus talked about with his Father is our destiny as well. That's what we were made for. . . .The heart and soul experience tragic assault in this war. The two essential categories needing ministry are wounding and brokenness—as we explore these you will understand why I draw a distinction between the two. But whatever the damage may be, however it was inflicted, however unreachable it might seem, the essence of healing prayer is always bringing the presence of Jesus into the afflicted places, for we are restored through union with him. I am reemphasizing this because sometimes the technicalities draw us away from the simplicity of this type of prayer; I want to make it readily accessible to you (pages 192–194).

» This is a good place to pause and reflect. Is *union with God* something you are seeking on a regular basis? Do you understand this to be the goal of your Christian life? Why or why not?

The loss of a father—or rejection by your father, abandonment, abuse—these are all wounds to the heart and soul. As are the same sorrows coming through a mother, or the absence of a mother. Or a brother, sister, coach, friend, lover, stranger. Think of wounding as taking an arrow to the heart and soul. It can come in so many ways: shame, guilt, betrayal, violation, neglect. The list is nearly endless, and growing more and more extreme as the world spirals deeper into darkness. Do not diminish the wounds you have received because you have heard far "worse" stories than yours; minimizing the impact of a wound never heals it. Jesus cares about it all (pages 194–195).

» Are you aware that your heart and soul have been wounded over the course of your life? Can you name a few of those significant wounds?

» How have you typically handled those wounds?

In the spirit of "there is a way things work," the basic approach for healing prayer typically goes like this:

- inviting the presence of Jesus into the wound specifically
- forgiving the one who wounded
- renouncing the message, the lie, breaking any agreement with it
- inviting the presence and healing love of God there (page 195).

» How did each of these steps play into the story I told about "Tami" in this chapter?

> You can probably relate to what I am describing. Certain places make you feel like a child again when you return there—your childhood home, or bedroom, a grade school, the location of a long forgotten family vacation. Perhaps you have also had the experience of suddenly feeling very young inside when a certain trigger happens—a song, or sound, even smells; someone gets angry with you, or touches you, or betrays you as an adult. Perhaps there are memories in which you feel like you are still six years old, or whatever age it was while you were there. However we encounter it, often it does feel as though there are young places within us. And there are (pages 197–198).

» Have you had the experiences I describe here? If so, how do they come to you? When do they happen? What seems to trigger them?

> However you choose to describe it, the reality . . . is that most of us have younger places within us that need the healing ministry of Jesus. A wound does not necessarily result in this brokenness, this fragmentation; wounds do pierce us, painfully, but some events actually shatter part of our inner being and that broken part remains at the age when the event took place (page 199).

» How am I differentiating a "wound" from "brokenness" within us? What characterizes "brokenness?"

> The "undivided heart" is what we are after. As with healing prayer for woundedness, we begin by inviting Jesus in. We ask him to shine his light into the broken places he is trying to reach. Sometimes he will take us back to a memory, a time and place when a shattering blow was given. Sometimes he will simply make us aware of a "young" place in our heart, a younger "us" that needs his love and comfort. Pay attention. Keep inviting Christ in (page 200).

» What is "step one" in healing brokenness, as I have described here?

> We ask Jesus what he is saying to this broken place within us. Jesus will often speak words of love or comfort to this specific young part of our heart. Sometimes he will ask us a question, like, *Why are you sad?* or *Why are you frightened?* Often he will ask, *Will you let me come to you?* Remember, he says he stands at the door and knocks, waiting for us to open the door for him to come in (Revelation 3:20). He waits for our permission to come and heal. Quite often these broken places "hide" behind the older parts of our personality, and that is why Jesus lovingly and gently invites them to come forward by asking questions (page 200).

» What is "step two" in healing brokenness, as I describe above?

As with wounding, [healing brokenness] often includes forgiving the ones who hurt us and releasing them to Jesus
(pages 200–201).

» And what does "step three" involve?

Self-rejection plays a major role here. It is quite common
for the older part of us to feel embarrassment, or anger,
or shame about the younger "stuck" place. And therefore
common for us to express rejection toward this part of us.
We push it away, push it to the background. That is why it
is important for us to renounce all self-rejection also, for
Jesus cannot integrate us while we are rejecting these
places within us (page 201).

» Summarize what I describe here as "step four."

The enemy will often use places of wounding as occasions
to oppress us; the same holds true for brokenness. In fact,
it is more common to find spiritual warfare in broken places
because the chasm in the heart and soul provides a place

for the enemy to do his work. He is a divider, after all; his main work is to divide—man from God, man from one another, and man from himself. So as we seek integration, we ask Jesus to bring his sword against the enemies that are "holding back" the young places, or oppressing them in some way (page 201).

» So, what is involved in "step five"?

We then ask Jesus for *integration*—to restore us in wholeheartedness, to heal up the brokenness and make us whole again, through his presence within us. We ask him to bring the young place into that wonderful home Jesus has made for himself in our hearts (Ephesians 3:17). The young parts of us feel safe with Jesus there; it is a place filled with love. And in that place Jesus can bring healing about, either in a moment or sometimes over time (pages 201–202).

» In the final step for inner healing, we ask Jesus to do what for us?

Physical Healing

» Turning our attention to chapter 16, what are the steps I laid out for physical healing prayer? Can you list them here?

Step One: Consecrate the . . .

Step Two: Invoke the . . .

Step Three: Give it . . .

Step Four: Watch for the . . .

Step Five: Address the . . .

Step Six: Curse the . . .

THE BIG IDEAS

» The essence of healing prayer is to bring the presence of Jesus into the afflicted places, for we are restored through union with him.

» Healing prayer involves inviting Jesus in, asking him to address our area of brokenness, forgiving those who hurt us, renouncing self-rejection, asking Christ to bring his sword against the enemy, and asking him to restore us to wholeness.

» Prayers for physical healing involve consecration, invoking the life of God, giving it time, watching for changes, addressing the demonic, and cursing the illness.

GROUP DISCUSSION

Watch the video for session seven. If you find it helpful, use the following space to take a few notes on anything that stands out to you.

Teaching Notes

DISCUSSION QUESTIONS

After the teaching session has ended, discuss as a group any or all of the following questions.

1. Read **James 5:14–15.** How did members of the early church view prayers for healing? What instructions does James give in this passage?

2. Read **Romans 12:1.** In prayer for physical healing, we bring the power of the resurrected Jesus into the afflicted body. How does consecration of the body play a role in this? Why is it important for the person with the affliction to pray for this?

3. After being sure the afflicted person is not making "agreements" with the enemy, we invoke the power of the resurrected Jesus into the person's body. In doing this, it is helpful to quote scriptures that remind us of the power and availability of God. What are some specific passages that come to mind?

4. The heart and soul can be wounded just like the body. Read
   Luke 2:34–35. What did Simeon say about the wound Mary
   would receive? Why did he phrase it in this way?

5. What do **Proverbs 12:18** and **Psalm 109:22** reveal about the
   inner wounds we receive?

6. What promises do we find in **Psalm 23:1–3, Psalm 147:3,** and
   Isaiah 61:1 about God's healing for our brokenness? Why is it
   significant that Jesus quoted this prophecy from Isaiah when
   he began his ministry (see **Luke 4:17–21**)?

7. What does it mean that "our soul is healed through union with
   Christ"? How did Jesus pray regarding our union with God in
   John 17:20–23?

PRAYER EXERCISE

Practicing inner healing prayer is worth every moment you put into it! We are talking about your *heart and soul*—the most important parts of you! So this is a form of prayer you are going to want to learn and mature in. It isn't necessary, but it often helps to have a close friend, pastor, or counselor pray with you if available. But again, this is *not* a requirement; I have experienced much healing with only Jesus by my side.

Let me strongly encourage you to first watch one of the free videos on our website at www.ransomedheart.com. Under the RHTV tab you will find a category called "live talks." In that library, you can watch "Captivating Live: Session 4—Healing the Wound" for women; for men, I recommend "Boot Camp Live: Session Four—The Wound." For healing brokenness, women can watch "Captivating Advanced: Session 3—Deeper Healing"; and for men, "Advanced Boot Camp: Session Three—The Wound and Healing." There are guided times of healing prayer in each of these videos.

HOLDING THE HEART IN UNANSWERED PRAYER

Friends, we are maturing. I need to call upon that maturity now,
to hold two things that seem opposite before you. Massive amounts of
healing, restoration, goodness, and beauty are available to us as we
take mature prayer seriously. But not every prayer will bring the
outcome you want, and what will you do with that? I think we need to
put all of this within a higher and greater context; I believe
that will help us, profoundly.

J O H N   E L D R E D G E

PERSONAL PREPARATION

» For this final week, read chapter 17 in *Moving Mountains:* "Holding the Heart in Every Outcome." Begin with your reaction to the chapter. What did these closing thoughts stir in you?

» At the beginning of chapter 17, I relate the story of a recent trip Stasi and I took to Hawaii.

> Now, I was very aware while I sat there in the stormy islands that our dear friend was still lying in a hospital bed in Houston, his battle with cancer taking a terrible toll—not only on his body, soul, and spirit, but on his spouse, family, and friends. I was very aware that the daughter of other friends was still on the streets, breaking her parents' hearts. A young man we care about was still in a state of mental illness; our sweet adopted daughter faced another year alone. I was very, *very* aware of the unanswered prayers all around us. These are the moments we must "guard our hearts," as Scripture urges:
>
>> Above all else, guard your heart,
>>   for it is the wellspring of life (Proverbs 4:23).
>
> Never was this more urgently needed than in the cases of unanswered prayer. We tried it; we went out on a limb; we put our hopes in God. Now what are we to do? It can feel like free-falling into the abyss (*Moving Mountains*, pages 216–217).

What unanswered prayers have been particularly hard for you, personally?

First—be *very* careful how you interpret "unanswered prayer." Our hearts are so vulnerable in these moments. It's just too easy to lose heart. The conclusions come rushing in—*God isn't listening; he doesn't care; I'm not faithful enough; prayer doesn't really work.* Catch yourself! Don't let your heart go there! Ask Jesus to help you interpret what is going on. *Jesus—catch my heart,* is the first thing I always pray. *Catch my heart, Lord. Help me interpret what is going on here.* Beware those nasty, soul-killing agreements (page 217).

» How have you been interpreting your unanswered prayers? Can you see "agreements" getting in? What have those unanswered prayers caused you to believe about God? About yourself? About prayer?

The disappointment of unanswered prayer can be devastating. We need to invite the love of God into the disappointment; we need his ministry there. We may need to shed some tears; we may need to grieve; we might need to take a baseball bat to a trashcan. However we express our heartsickness, we *must* invite Jesus there—just like we do with inner healing prayer—to comfort, heal, and restore (page 217).

» Have you done this? If so, what was the result?

> I have had to add another phrase to my journal on who
> God is, and who I am:
>
>> God is not a betrayer—he does not betray and
>> he has never betrayed me.
>
> Because unanswered prayer that was urgent and
> beyond precious to you can feel like a knife to the heart.
> The enemy rushes in with feelings of betrayal; he whispers
> terrible things about God in our vulnerability. It is never,
> ever true. But sometimes I have to remind myself of that
> (pages 216–217).

» Has a sense that God has betrayed you crept in through your
disappointment and heartache? If so, how will you pause and
break those agreements even now?

> The Son of God is the sower; he says so himself. He then
> honestly admits that even *his* efforts prevail only some
> of the time. Not all of the time—some of the time. One in
> four. Jesus implies that his batting average is about .250.
> And this is *Jesus* we are talking about—the man who walked
> on water, calmed the storm, fed five thousand, raised

Lazarus and a few other people from the dead. What do you make of that? You are going to have to come to terms with the partial nature of this life. Have you come to terms yet with the partial? (page 219).

» Have you come to terms with this? How are you currently handling the "partial" nature of this life?

Paul saw some pretty staggering answers to prayer as he fought for the beachhead that was early Christianity. He healed people; he cast out demons; he brought salvation to thousands; he raised the dead. But he was also stoned and left for dead; he was shipwrecked three times; five times he received the "thirty-nine lashes" (once was supposed to kill a man); he faced many sleepless nights; he knew exposure, hunger, and cold. And remember—*all of heaven was committed to this man being successful.* His life was magnificent, powerful, triumphant. But no, Paul did not try and make his life like retirement in Hawaii (page 220).

» What do you do with these types of stories from the Scriptures? All of heaven was committed to Paul's success, and he *was* successful! But he also knew a great deal of heartache. What do you do with that truth?

Dear ones, our real class work has just begun. God is growing us all up. The goal of that maturity—much to our surprise—is not a life free from affliction. Not yet. There is something even greater than happiness, something far higher he has for us (page 221).

» How does this idea sit with the way you live your life? I don't mean your theology—I mean your day-to-day commitments and "under the surface" beliefs.

God is weaning us to the place we will be able to say like David, "Your love is better than life" (Psalm 63:3), to truly and actually believe in the marrow of our bones that God's love surpasses anything this world has to offer. To find Jesus Christ as our absolute all-in-all. To be able to say with Paul, "For to me, to live is Christ and to die is gain" (Philippians 1:21). And how did Paul learn that most precious of all lessons? "I consider everything a loss because of the surpassing worth of knowing Christ Jesus my Lord, for whose sake I have lost all things" (Philippians 3:8 UPDATED NIV). He learned it through loss; he learned it through suffering. This is what the men and women who speak of God after years of profound suffering have to say. This is the most beautiful form of holiness; God has become everything to them. And dear friends—God is deeply committed to shaping this very holiness in us. This is the outcome of the maturity we have been talking about (pages 223–224).

» Is this the goal of your maturity? What do you honestly do with what I have said here?

The mighty victory is staying true to God. It is maintaining a mature perspective—where God means everything to you—through glorious breakthrough and in the midst of terrible affliction. If you do not hold fast to this, you will be shaken when your prayers do not seem to prevail; you will fall prey to feelings of failure or despair. Or, you will be grasping at promises of unending victory, looking down on those who do not see things as you do. You will be forced to ignore the sufferings of Christ, and our honor in sharing in them. And you will miss the goal of this life, which is not unending breakthrough, but something far more beautiful and everlasting—the beauty of Jesus Christ, which your Father is committed to forming in you: "God knew what he was doing from the very beginning. He decided from the outset to shape the lives of those who love him along the same lines as the life of his Son. The Son stands first in the line of humanity he restored. We see the original and intended shape of our lives there in him" (Romans 8:29 MSG) (pages 227–228).

» React to this, honestly.

» In the chapter, I write how after the last embers of the Waldo Canyon Fire finally died out, I would walk up in the hills behind our house to survey the devastation. I stopped taking those walks after a while. But when I did return to the hills the next summer:

> Wildflowers were blooming here, there, *everywhere*—happy little lavender asters, absurdly tall and joyful sunflowers, blood-red Indian paintbrush, clusters of purple penstemon. In greater abundance than I had ever seen before. The deep-rooted yuccas had survived and were shooting up with vigor, as was all the scrub oak. The wild grasses had grown waist high, swaying like a green sea in the light breezes. Someone had washed the land with so much color and life it looked like a Van Gogh painting. We have staked it all on this—that life wins. Oh dear friends—*life wins*. Life wins. Sometimes now, especially if we will pray. But life wins fully, and very soon. Just as we must fix our eyes on Jesus when we pray, we must also fix our hearts on this one undeniable truth: life *will* win (pages 228–229).

Is your heart fixed on this great promise of our faith? Explain.

> We cry out for [Jesus'] return and the restoration of all things. "Come back—Jesus, come back," ought to flow naturally and passionately off your lips every day. (If it doesn't, might it be a sign you are looking to arrange for your life here?) (page 229)

» Do you cry out for the return of Christ on a regular basis? If not . . . why not?

> "Pour out your Spirit, Jesus!" We pray for one last great harvest, like fire fighters rescuing every last life they can from a building about to collapse in flames. I love these prayers because they have nothing to do with my immediate life, my struggles. They call me up into a larger story, lift my eyes to the more important things. It's so refreshing not to always be praying for the crisis before me (page 230).

» How will you add these last two prayers—for a last great harvest and for the return of Jesus—to your regular prayer focus?

» In closing, what would you say have been the biggest "aha!" moments for you in this study?

» What are the biggest new "tools" for prayer you are walking away with?

THE BIG IDEAS

» We have to be careful how we interpret "unanswered prayer."
» We must come to terms with the partial nature of this life and admit that we won't always receive our desired answers to prayer.
» The goal of this life is not unending breakthrough but the beauty of Christ, which God is committed to forming within us.

GROUP DISCUSSION

Watch the video for session eight. If you find it helpful, use the following space to take a few notes on anything that stands out to you.

Teaching Notes

DISCUSSION QUESTIONS

After the teaching session has ended, discuss as a group any or all of the following questions.

1. Read **Matthew 13:3–8.** What happens to the different kinds of "seeds" in this parable? What does Jesus, the Sower, say about the results of his own efforts?

2. We have to be careful about how we *interpret* unanswered prayer. Read **Genesis 3:1–5.** What does this passage tell us about how our enemy tries to twist the truth of our situation and get us to question God's intentions?

3. When we do not receive an answer to prayer, it is important for us to ask Jesus for his interpretation. What promise are we given in **James 1:5** when we seek godly wisdom? What does Paul pray for the believers in **Ephesians 1:17–18**?

4. Remember how Elijah prayed for rain (see **1 Kings 18:41–46**) and the early church prayed for Peter's release (see **Acts 12:1–18**). What does this tell us about keeping at it when we don't immediately get the answer we seek? What do we need to remember about the spiritual warfare taking place around us when we pray?

5. There is a time for contending, but there is also a time to let go. How will we know when this time has come? What enables us to receive this discernment?

6. God says one day he will wipe every tear from our eyes and the life we dreamed of will be ours (see **Revelation 21:4**). In the meantime, what is our goal in this life? How does centering our lives on God's purposes keep us from being shaken when we don't receive the answers we desire?

7. Read **1 Peter 4:13** and **2 Corinthians 1:5.** What does it mean to share in the sufferings of Christ? What is God's ultimate purpose for us when we go through trials?

PRAYER EXERCISE

If you or your group would like to go further, I would recommend diving into some of the fabulous resources at www.ransomed heart.com. I mentioned the videos available through the RHTV tab, which are designed to take you deeper into discipleship in Jesus and his kingdom. We also have small group studies available. For further reading, I would encourage you to read through *Waking the Dead, Beautiful Outlaw,* or *Free to Live.* I hope you've enjoyed this study as much as I enjoyed writing it for you!

LEADER'S GUIDE

Thank you for your willingness to lead a group through *Moving Mountains: Praying with Passion, Confidence, and Authority.* The rewards of leading are different from the rewards of participating, and we hope you find your own walk with Jesus deepened by this experience. This leader's guide will give you some tips on how to prepare for your time together and faciliate a meaningful experience for your group members.

What Does It Take to Lead This Study?

Get together and watch God show up. Seriously, that's the basics of how a small group works. Gather several people who have a hunger for God, want to learn how to pray more effectively, and are willing to be open and honest with God and themselves. God will honor this every time and show up in the group. You don't have to be a pastor, priest, theologian, or counselor to lead a group through this study. Just invite people over, watch the video, and talk about it. All you need is a willing heart, a little courage, and God will do the rest. Really.

How This Study Works

There are three important pieces to the *Moving Mountains* small group study: (1) the book *Moving Mountains,* (2) the eight-session video, and (3) this study guide. Make sure everyone in your group has a copy of the book and a study guide. It works best if you can get books and guides to your group *before* the first meeting. That way, everyone can read the first two chapters ahead of time and be prepared to watch the first video session together.

This series is presented in eight video sessions, with each session approximately twelve minutes in length. Each week, you'll meet together to watch the video and discuss the session. (You can also watch two sessions per week if you prefer to meet together for only four weeks, though this will require the group members to read four chapters of the book each week.) This series can also be used in classroom settings, such as Sunday school classes, though you may need to modify the discussion time depending on the size of the class. You could even use the video as sessions for a special prayer retreat.

Basically, each week you and your group will: (1) read the corresponding chapters in *Moving Mountains*, (2) answer a few pre-session questions found in this guide, (3) watch one of the video sessions together, and (4) talk about it. That's it!

A Few Tips for Leading a Group

The setting really matters. If you can choose to meet in a living room over a conference room in a church, do it. Pick an environment that's conducive to people relaxing and getting real. Remember the enemy likes to distract us when it comes to prayer and seeking God, so do what you can to remove these obstacles from your group (silence cell phones, limit background noise, no texting). Set the chairs or couches in a circle to prevent having a "classroom" feel.

Have some refreshments! Coffee and water will do; cookies and snacks are even better. People tend to be nervous when they join a new group, so if you can give them something to hold onto (like a warm mug of coffee), they will relax a lot more. It's human nature.

Good equipment is important. Meet where you can watch the video sessions on a screen big enough for everyone to see and enjoy. Get or borrow the best gear you can. Also, be sure to test your media equipment ahead of time to make sure everything is in working condition. This way, if something isn't working, you can fix it or make other arrangements before the meeting begins. (You'll be amazed at how the enemy will try to mess things up for you!)

Be honest. Remember that your honesty will set the tone for your time together. Be willing to answer questions personally, as this will set the pace for the length of people's responses and will make others more comfortable in sharing.

Stick to the schedule. Strive to begin and end at the same time each week. The people in your group are busy, and if they can trust you to be a good steward of their time, they will be more willing to come back each week. Of course, you want to be open to the work God is doing in people as they learn new aspects of prayer they might not have understood before, and at times you will want to *linger* in prayer. The clock serves *you;* your group doesn't serve the clock. But work to respect the group's time, especially when it comes to limiting the discussion times.

Don't be afraid of silence or emotion. Welcome awkward moments. Most people are nervous when it comes to talking about their prayer life, their struggles, and the stumbles they have in their relationship with God. Ease into it. By week three or four you'll be humming along.

Don't dominate the conversation. Even though you are the leader, you are also a member of this small group. So don't steamroll over others in an attempt to lead—and don't let anyone else in the group do so either.

Prepare for your meeting. Watch the video for the meeting ahead of time. Though it may feel a bit like cheating because you'll know what's coming, you'll be better prepared for what the session might stir in the hearts of your group members. Also review the material in this guide and be sure to spend time in prayer. In fact, the *most important* thing you can do is simply pray ahead of time each week:

> Lord Jesus, come and rule this time. Let your Spirit fill this place. Bring your kingdom here. Take us right to the things we really need to talk about and rescue us from every distraction. Show us the heart of the Father. Meet each

person here. Give us your grace and love for one another. In your name I pray.

Make sure your group members are prepared. Before the first meeting, secure enough copies of the study guide and the *Moving Mountains* book for each member. Have these ready and on hand for the first meeting, or make sure the participants have purchased these resources for themselves. Send out a reminder email or a text a couple of days before the meeting to make sure folks don't forget about it.

As You Gather

You will find the following counsel to be especially helpful when you meet for the first time as a group. I offer these comments in the spirit of "here is what I would do if I were leading a group through this study."

First, as the group gathers, start your time with introductions if people don't know each other. Begin with yourself and share your name, how long you've been a follower of Christ, if you have a spouse and/or children, and what you want to learn most about the power and effectiveness of prayer. Going first will put the group more at ease.

After each person has introduced himself or herself, share—in no more than five minutes—what your hopes are for the group. Then jump right into watching the video session, as this will help get things started on a strong note. In the following weeks you will then want to start by allowing folks to catch up a little—say, fifteen minutes or so—with some "hey, so how are you?" kind of banter. Too much of this burns up your meeting time, but you have to allow some room for it because it helps build relationships among the group members.

Note that each group will have its own personality and dynamics. Typically, people will hold back the first week or two until they feel the group is "safe." Then they will begin to share. Again, don't let it throw you if your group seems a bit awkward at first. Of course, some people *never* want to talk, so you'll need to coax them out as time goes on. But let it go the first week.

Insight for Discussion

If the group members are in any way open to talking about their lives as it relates to this material on prayer, you will *not* have enough time for every question suggested in this study guide. That's okay! Pick the questions ahead of time that you know you want to cover, just in case you end up only having time to discuss a few of them.

You set the tone for the group. Your honesty and vulnerability during discussion times will tell them what they can share. How *long* you talk will give them an example of how long they should. So give some thought to what stories or insights from your own work in the study guide you want to highlight.

WARNING: The greatest temptation for most small group leaders is to add to the video teaching with a little "teaching session" of their own. This is unhelpful for three reasons:

1. The discussion time will be the richest time during your meeting. The video sessions have been intentionally kept short so you can have plenty of time for discussion. If you add to the teaching, you sacrifice this precious time.

2. You don't want your group members "teaching" or "lecturing" or "correcting" one another. Every person is at a different place in his or her spiritual journey when it comes to prayer—and that's good. But if you set a tone by teaching, the group will feel like they have the freedom to teach one another. That can be disastrous for group dynamics.

3. The participants will have read the corresponding chapters in *Moving Mountains,* done the preparation work in this guide, and watched the video. They don't need more content! They want a chance to talk and process their own lives in light of all they have taken in.

A Strong Close

Some of the best learning times will take place after the group time as God brings new insights to the participants during the week. Encourage group members to write down any questions they have as they read through *Moving Mountains* and do the preparation work and weekly prayer exercises. Make sure they know you are available for them, especially as they get into the deeper chapters on spiritual warfare, prayers for physical and inner healing, and dealing with unanswered prayers.

Finally, make sure you close your time by—*praying together!* Perhaps ask two or three people to pray, inviting God to fill your group and lead each person during this study. Also, be sure to "practice" some of the specific prayers your group will be learning about during the sessions. Many of these prayers can be found in the corresponding chapters to the sessions or in the appendix of *Moving Mountains.*

Thank you again for taking the time to lead your group. May God reward your efforts and dedication and make your time together in *Moving Mountains* fruitful for his kingdom.

RANSOMED HEART'S
FREE GIFT TO YOU

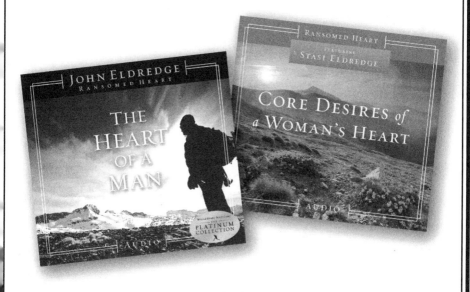

Recorded live, these powerful messages from John and Stasi Eldredge speak to the core desires of the male and female heart. Choose one or both full-length audio downloads.

Visit RansomedHeart.com, click to the Store page, and input the audio title you want (*The Heart of a Man* and/or *Core Desires of a Woman's Heart*). At checkout, type the code HEART and you will receive one or both audio downloads at no charge.

RANSOMED HEART
LOVE GOD. LIVE FREE.

THERE IS SO MUCH MORE

When people think about Ransomed Heart, some connect it solely with John Eldredge's books—or perhaps with the live events in Colorado.

But there is so much more.

This 54-minute free download is the ideal resource for all who want to know more about the heart of Ransomed Heart Ministries.

Available exclusively at RansomedHeart.com.

RANSOMED HEART

LOVE GOD. LIVE FREE.